Minecraft: Creative Handbook

Ultimate Minecraft Creation Guide

Table of Contents

Introduction

Minecraft is among the most beloved games on the ever since it was launched.

Minecraft has become widely popular in the gaming world due to its creative and visually appealing features.

The idea of being able to mine, and then craft not only structures, but practically whole virtual worlds of your own, has made it extremely attractive to anyone looking for an outlet for their creativity.

Minecraft has sold over 30 million copies, a number which increases daily owing to its ever increasing popularity.

While simple in design, Minecraft offers five different game modes, which makes it easy to pick and choose a mode which suits you best.

Among the game modes, you get, you can choose from:

- Creative,

- Survival,

- Adventure,

- Spectator,

- Hardcore.

While Minecraft players who are looking for a challenge usually choose other worlds, if you want to simply build or are new to the game, the creative mode will be the best option for you.

With the help of this eBook, we're going to show how easy it is to build and play and let your creativity in the Minecraft Creative mode.

Basics of Creative Mode

When creating your world in creative mode, you get

the option of choosing to have a flat land surface or

a biome one as well as choosing to have the day

night cycle or experiencing constant day in your

game.

Once you've chosen the options which suit you the best, it is time to start building.

When you start out in Creative mode, you are going to have a full inventory. Every block in Minecraft will already be available for your building ease.

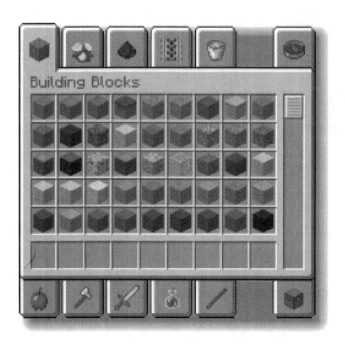

Apart from the blocks, you will also get eggs with which you can spawn any mob or monster in Minecraft as well.

Another feature which you will enjoy is that there are no mobs or monsters which could disturb you.

Now that you've got the problems for materials out of the way, you can start to focus on the beginning to build.

Getting Creative in Minecraft

Minecraft is an easy game to get creative with. Because you can build almost anything in Minecraft, you can get inspiration from anything.

Look at architectural structures around you for inspiration. You can incorporate any style of building whether you want a modern, medieval gothic or just a simple monument.

Luckily, you don't have to be limited to things around you. You can rebuild a fantasy castle from any book or game that you like.

For example: You can make a castle from the Lord

of the Rings

Or even some other mythical castle

Doing Some Research

Once you've chosen the kind of build you want to

make, do a little research on it.

Even if you're trying to build a fantasy castle, based on the description given in a book, you will still need to get an idea of how castles should look.

First things first, you have to think about what kind

of house or structure you want to build. Think of a

theme and do a little research to get inspiration.

If you want to build castles then their layouts and anything else that you want to add to your own castle.

The more clearly you picture and study your house,

the better you will be able to reproduce it.

Minecraft Physics and Gravity

Keep in mind that Minecraft integrates most laws of Physics, Chemistry and the gravitational pull of the Earth.

This means that just like in real life, making a flimsy

or lopsided house in Minecraft with a poor design

or poor materials will cause it to fall or cave in.

This means a loss of time and energy so doing some

extra research will pay off.

Blueprints

Try to find blue prints of buildings that you want to

make.

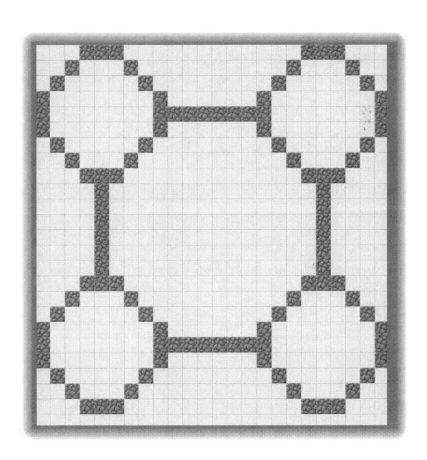

This will help you plan the layout and give you a good idea regarding room placements and how to incorporate different features into the build.

Doing a little research you can allow you to make almost any kind of creative build in Minecraft.

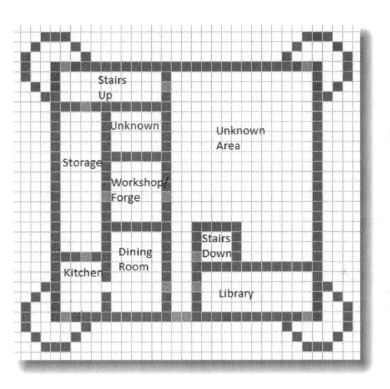

Remember that your first house in Minecraft may not be the best one you make.

Luckily, your skills at building will just get better and better so have patience and do not get disheartened.

Decorating the Exterior

Make the wall with two different materials integrated together.

This breaks the monotony by giving the eye some variety to look at. This also cuts down on the amount of material need to make it.

Windows are useful in allowing you to look out at the oncoming enemy and you can make them by putting in one glass block.

However, small windows are not very pleasing to look at and you can easily combine three or more blocks to make larger windows which are more pleasing to eye and allow you more visibility outside.

Give the wall shape and trim according to the kind

of house you are making.

If you are making a castle, turrets and other ledges

are common for the wall to have.

This also gives the walls more depth, texture and helps to give authenticity to the nature of your building.

Decorating the Interior

The interior of the house does not have to be monotonous either. Like the exterior of the house, using double materials can add more texture to the walls.

But you can go one step further by adding double texture floors and ceilings. This adds more depth and looks better in your house too.

Once you're done with that, let's move on to the nitty gritty details of the house. You have to add torches, everywhere.

This makes the mobs reluctant to approach your house and eliminates their chances of accidentally spawning in your house.

You can place torches anywhere or make special

niches for them using some fencing.

Among the furniture items, the bed, chests, paintings and the bookshelf are the only ones which are easily buildable; you will have to be imaginative with other items.

Use the stair block to make sofas and the pressure plates along with some fencing to create some tables.

You can even introduce levers, pressure plate operated controls and other redstone circuitry across the house to have a somewhat automated house hold.

Finally to complete the ambiance, add bookshelves,

paintings, a few chests and furnaces and you're

done!

Using Your Blue Prints

Once you've studied the area and decided on how many rooms, and what kind of structure you want to build, it's time to lay down a blue print with blocks.

Doing so, you will be able to build in a more controlled manner and it will help you to allot the right amount space to all the rooms you want.

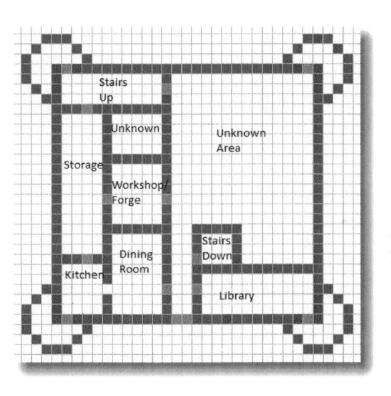

This also prevents you from accidentally forgetting about a certain room for feature you would have wanted in your house.

Even if you are not making something huge, laying down an outline can help bring more perspective to your building.

Start Small

Many people in Minecraft love the idea of building a huge mansion, castle or other monuments of huge proportions.

These things are easier thought off and really hard to do. It takes a lot of planning, resources, time and patience to get the end result.

If you chose to start such a big build, you might become bored and abandon it before it is complete.

That is why start with something small and build

your expertise till you can understand and have the

time and patience to invest in bigger builds.

Think Out of the Box

When building, don't try to cram everything into one building.

With an open sandbox realm, you have plenty of space at your disposal and you can create different buildings for different purposes.

Just remember to space them near your house but

not to near to avoid giving a cramped air.

Similarly, don't space too far apart, this could both

be tiresome and cause you to encounter mobs on

your way to these places.

Now that we've discussed these tips, here are a few

ideas on what to build next:

A storage room

A room dedicated entirely to storing your items where you can store as many chests as you can.

A Treasury

Purely to allow you to gloat, a treasury can house all your valuables. Use precious metals in the walls of the room to follow the treasury's theme.

A Blacksmith's Forge

This room can be stacked full of furnaces and act as

a production room.

Farms, Sugar cane Farms, Pastures and Barns

These help you to gain food and animal related resources in bulk. Make these only when you have found a spot to settle permanently in.

An Underwater home

With the ocean biome, you can now build

magnificent underwater domes for yourself.

Gather wood blocks, swim down to the bottom of your ocean biome and build a mound of 20x 20 blocks. Do not to make them hollow like you would if you were building above water.

Once you have a sturdy building made of wood, you can layer glass blocks around the wooden structure.

Burn wood blocks leaving a glass hut

Now, start digging right under the glass to reach the wood. Leave a gap of one block and work your way under that, starting at the second block.

When you reach the wood, set it on fire and the wood blocks will burn, leaving a glass dome or room that is waterproof.

Made in the USA
Middletown, DE
18 October 2016